How a Seed Grows

by Holly Schroeder
illustrated by Denny Bond

Scott Foresman
is an imprint of

Glenview, Illinois • Boston, Massachusetts • Chandler, Arizona
Upper Saddle River, New Jersey

Illustrations
Denny Bond

ISBN 13: 978-0-328-50852-5
ISBN 10:   0-328-50852-7

10 V010 15 14

seed

This is a seed. Seeds can have different colors and textures. Some seeds grow into flowers or trees. Some seeds are grains like corn or wheat.

A seed sprouts.

This seed may become a flower.
First, the seed must sprout. To *sprout*
means to "start growing."

soil

This is soil. Soil is a material that plants need to grow. Seeds sprout in soil.

Seeds need different substances.
Seeds will not grow without water.
Water seeps through the soil to the seed.

← root

This is a root. Roots keep the plant in the soil. Roots bring water and healthy particles to the plant.

seedling →

This is a seedling. Seedlings grow out of the seed. It will grow toward the sun.

The seedling grows. The plant turns green.

flower →

This is a flower. Soil, water, and sun help the plant grow. Then a flower opens, or blooms. Flowers make a plant look beautiful.

The flower drops seeds onto
the ground. Some seeds will grow
into new flowers. This is the most
amazing process in nature.

Follow the diagram that shows the seed being planted. What do you think happens next?